simply chaos

Sara Maccombs

BookLeaf Publishing

Presentation by *BookLeaf Publishing*

Web: www.bookleafpub.com

E-mail: info@bookleafpub.com

ISBN: 9789357210249

First edition 2022

DEDICATION

to the ones who can't find the words to explain their feelings

my beautiful sister, who reminds me to follow my dreams

my sweetest grandma, who thought i was perfect without fault

my amazing, graceful, and beautiful mom, who loved me regardless of my faults

believed in me before i knew how to believe in myself

and who to this day will be my biggest supporter

i miss you everyday

ACKNOWLEDGEMENT

ash and kourt, for celebrating every win and loss with me

charlie, for being a queen and doing the cover

jen, for believing in me when i forgot to believe in myself

my nieces, who remind me everyday that to be a strong woman doesn't always mean being the toughest person in the room

PREFACE

it took me years to learn to love my own words
years to understand that all of the jumbled mess
of words that was scrambled in my mind, could
turn into something
and to learn to simply love the chaos of it

my beacon

i remember it was the moon
that i thought of the day you left
but when the moon disappears
it's always just to rest

there was something that drew me to it
even in the darkest night it would glow
like it's the beacon of the sky
to everyone down below

and now i look up at it
and remember when you were mine
but now that you're gone
it's my beacon all the time

my worth

i question my worth
am i enough
does the moon ask it's worth when the sun rises
when the sun rises and brings a new day with it
the moon gives us rest for a new day so we can
grow
the moon is worth a new day
but what do i bring
am i enough
what am i worth

wild girl

this girl runs wild
like a river after a rain
her bare feet's always dirty
from letting her run free reign
but there's no stopping her
she just can't be detained

her love is easy
like a summer breeze
her curls hang wild
because she likes them to be free
there's patience in her
more than anyone I've ever seen

her smile's crooked
with dimples that pop out
and eyes as blue as the ocean
those are from grandpa no doubt
she's talks a mile a minute
about things she dreams about

she's tougher than a bull
and stubborn as can be
she's everything like you
and sometimes like me

i wish you could meet her
your great granddaughter you always dreamed

sister

laughing until 2am
sleeping in until noon
we go to together
like the sun and the moon

you brighten my darkness
while i bring the night
i understand why they always say
sisters are for life

hooked

he's handsome
in a way that's over looked
my heart beats faster
i've probably misunderstood
he doesn't see my smile
but i wish he would
i'm not sure how i got here
but i'm positive i'm already hooked

cold night

a thousand scattered words
fill my page

the emptiness of the night
increases my pain

coldness seeps in
from the midnight rain

why are some nights so brutal
while others seem tame

tonight i seek your comfort
can you hear me calling your name

the morning sun starts to rise
and lifts some of my strain

the warmth of the sunshine
somehow helps me feel sane

Lord you've answered my silent prayer
breaking my cold lonely chains

when we were young

back when we thought we had it all
starting new was fun
and we weren't afraid to fall

falling in love and living fast
never ones to second guess
and finding out not everything lasts

we fought hard to beat the odds
always living for ourselves
never for applause

finding ourselves in this life
knowing there's something more
that we wanted to strive for

grandma

your love ran deep
deeper than the ocean depth
your love was shared
shared with each breath
your love was my rock
holding me while i wept

your soul was beautiful
beautiful like a mountain rose
your soul had a fire
a fire that drew everyone close
your soul was pure
so pure i thought it would glow

your strength was breathtaking
breathtaking in full view
your strength to speak your mind
speaking your mind but never untrue
your strength held us all together
together through and through

so i want to thank you
for loving us a way that many desire
having a soul full of kindness most never know
and strength that will always be admired

home

home is where the heart is
but my heart is someplace else
searching for a place
that i saw on a book shelf

one place to the next
nothing seems to fit
i'm tired of this feeling
something's gotta shift

looking for some sort of answers
but there's nothing i can find
i settle into a new place
and hope i don't lose my mind

home is where the heart is
that much i know for sure
but my heart is set on new places
my home is out on tour

on my knees

i'm on my knees.
begging for forgiveness
crying out for Jesus
my life has turned around
and i'm too scared to let him down
so i'm grieving the life i had
with the love that kept away the bad

and i'm on my knees
begging for a chance
to make me stand
for him to turn me back around
and make me his child that he sent down

i'm on knees
begging for forgiveness
crying out for Jesus
knowing that i'm wrong
in more ways than one
begging you to take my hand
and guide me through my life
knowing i'm not perfect
and i'll cry out for a purpose

dance in the rain

seeing the ocean with it's blue depths
along the shore with my toes in the sand
i couldn't believe how free i felt
alone here where i stand

the thunder came loud and the rain started strong
but seeing the waves crashing
my soul felt it deep
i started to feel the passion

the constant emptiness i felt
starts to ease
the storm and the ocean
surrounds me with peace

life wasn't meant to be suffered through
i wasn't put here to complain
my mind was made up
i'd learn to dance in the rain

guiding me home

i made promises and i left them hang in the air
i did wrong even when i knew what was right
my mind wasn't thinking about much
just getting back in touch
with the life that i wanted
the life that i planned.
i fought against what you wanted
trying to make my own way
knowing i was wrong
but wanting it my way
you never left
just kept reminding me
of where i'd end up
my heart was beating out of my chest
knowing I'd chose the wrong path
but you grabbed me by the hand
and helped me stand
you didn't judge me for my mistakes
just helped me back to your saving grace
you never left me out there alone
you were always there guiding me home

mom

you beautiful person
i can’t comprehend
how God took you
and called it the end

your laugh dances forever
your love touches deep
your smile is etched in our memories
memories we’ll forever keep

our hearts feel so empty
our lives forever changed
you brought the sunshine
now all we feel is the rain

your battle is over
God assured you won
we’ll all miss you
love your husband, daughters, and son

wild and free

tell me what it's like
what it's like to be wild and free
to look into the sky and see no limits
everything's possible and you're not afraid to
leave

i've fallen in love with places i don't know
a mad desire to be any where but here
to see something that touches my soul
showing me everything in clear

the wildness of leaving
no matter how far
the freeness of being able to go
showing how passionate you are

there's a space in my heart
filled with a desire to go with the flow
to see everything
waiting for the day when i can pick up the pieces
and go

following your dreams instead of others to be
free
there's no finding the right time

stop caring what others are going to say to be
wild
and stop searching for the sign

three peas in a pod

it wasn't love at first sight
or anything like that
but the three of us instantly clicked
our souls all somehow matched

since day one
we've seen every flaw
but it's just like we say
we're three peas in a pod

you're there for my worst
and celebrate every win
you're my go to for everything
i can't even begin

three peas in a pod
until death do us part
no it wasn't love at first sight
but you're both forever a part of my heart

forever friend

growing older isn't as bad as i thought
friends and family grow older
and friendships grow longer
i find that the relationships grow stronger
the longer they're here
and ours was strengthened by calls
letters
and family get togethers

april showers

memories cling to me like fresh tattoos
of your old worn boots and southern roots

i can remember it all
it's clear in my mind, especially our downfall

the spring was fresh in the air
when i found you sitting there

a wide smile i hadn't seen in a while
you were flirting with her and i felt like I was
exiled

i should've believed when they said you never
cared
but i thought back then, that i needed you like air

when the april showers came down
that's when my whole world was turned around

when the lightning struck
and you started to self destruct

i stayed waiting for you
because i didn't know what else to do

it took a while to figure out
that i wasn't supposed to live in doubt

so when the april showers washed me clean
thankfully, there was no more you and me

feeling

maybe it's the way you see the world
you see it differently
feel it too deeply
but not everyone is going to see it like you
they won't feel like you
they won't care like you
you have to take it as it comes unfortunately
it's going to hurt
but you'll make it brighter
maybe not for you
but for them

nothing but you

did you see that look in her eyes
after you said goodbye

the tears rolled down her face
you had been her only escape

now wishing she had you back
she left right after she packed

she wanted nothing but you
but knew it would never be true

so she cried all alone
wishing you'd pick up the phone

because she knew what you said was true
that she'd ruined it all with you

no guidelines

i'm too much and yet not enough
my attitude sucks but i've had enough
the definition of a woman isn't clear
but for some people, you won't find her here

momma wanted me strong
to fight for what i want
but daddy wanted a little girl
who he could protect

i'm too loud for you
but i need to speak up
the way you think i need act
is just so you can get off

i can't be everything you want
i don't have to be
this world doesn't need more guidelines
so i'm just going to be me.

your love

i'm staggering for a place
for me to call home
i'm too scared to face
all of the unknown
i can't see anything clearly
so i call out and cry
"can you even hear me"
looking up toward the sky
and then your love comes washing down
you pull me up every time before i drown

www.ingramcontent.com/pod-product-compliance
Lightning Source LLC
Chambersburg PA
CBHW062110140826
49812CB00058B/1172
9789357210249